Contents

What a difference!

The main difference between birds and most other animals is their ability to fly.

Bird characteristics

- Birds are warm-blooded.
- Their bodies are covered in feathers.
- They have two wings.
- They use a beak to obtain food.
- They lay eggs to produce young.

The ostrich is ▶ the world's largest bird. Ostriches cannot fly because they are too heavy, sometimes weighing up to 156 kilograms.

Birds can be very different from each other. Some are large while others are tiny. Many birds have unusual beaks. Some have brilliantly coloured feathers.

The male bird of paradise has ▶ brightly coloured feathers to attract a female.

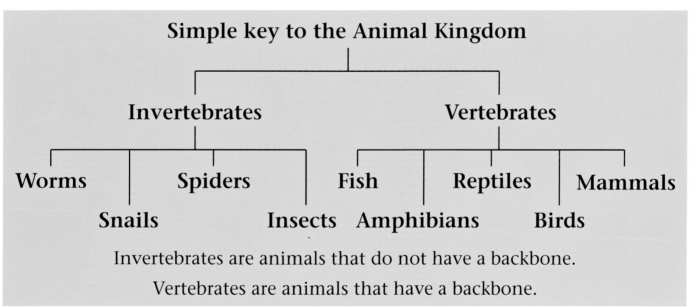

Simple key to the Animal Kingdom

Invertebrates   Vertebrates

Worms   Spiders   Fish   Reptiles   Mammals

Snails   Insects   Amphibians   Birds

Invertebrates are animals that do not have a backbone.
Vertebrates are animals that have a backbone.

Where birds live

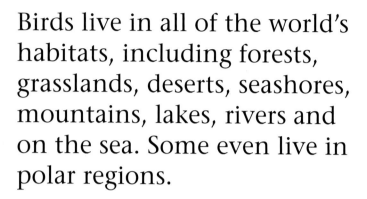

Birds live in all of the world's habitats, including forests, grasslands, deserts, seashores, mountains, lakes, rivers and on the sea. Some even live in polar regions.

Living in different habitats

- Forest and woodland birds have clawed feet for gripping branches.
- Ducks have webbed feet for swimming.
- Birds that live in water have waterproof feathers.
- Vultures have large wings for gliding over grassland.

◀ Snowy owls live in the frozen Arctic. Their white feathers keep them warm and camouflaged against the snow.

Birds have special features that help them to live in these very different habitats. These features include long legs, webbed and clawed feet, and beaks of different shapes.

◀ The tree creeper has large clawed feet for gripping bark. Its beak is curved for poking into holes in search of insects.

▲ This stilt has long legs for wading in shallow water and a long beak so it can reach food on the lake bottom.

Catching a meal

The shape of a bird's beak is a clue to the type of food it eats. Eagles have sharp beaks for tearing food into bite-sized pieces.

Parrots and finches use their strong beaks to crack open seeds and nuts, or scoop out fruit. A thin beak is good for catching insects.

▲ The kingfisher dives into the river to catch small fish.

◄ The pied wagtail eats insects that it catches on the ground or in the air.

▲ A parrot can hold a nut in its foot while breaking the shell with its tough beak.

Hawks and eagles have excellent eyesight to spot small mammals. They dive on their prey, grabbing it with their clawed feet.

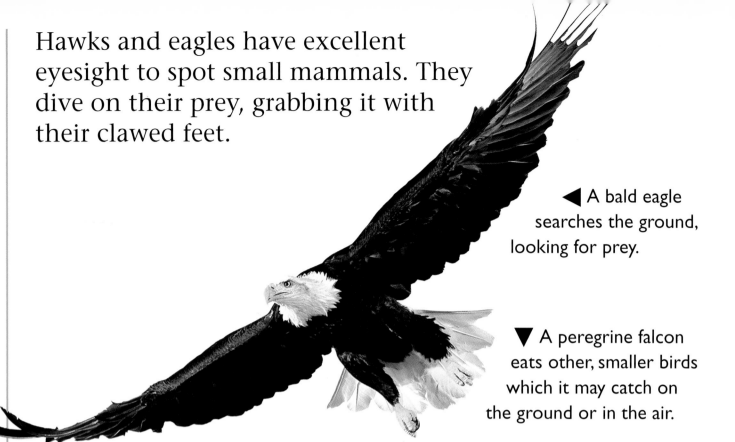

◀ A bald eagle searches the ground, looking for prey.

▼ A peregrine falcon eats other, smaller birds which it may catch on the ground or in the air.

A few birds use tools to catch food. The woodpecker finch holds a cactus spine in its beak to prise insects from holes in trees. The Egyptian vulture picks up stones with its beak and drops them onto ostrich eggs to break the shells.

Vultures feed on ▶ dead animals.

Avoiding predators

🐦 Female birds are usually brown, so they cannot easily be spotted on their nests.

🐦 The fulmar can spit foul liquid at an attacker.

🐦 Ducks and swans often sleep on water, where they are safe from attack.

Hot and cold

Birds have soft, fluffy feathers to keep them warm. They must bathe regularly to keep their feathers clean, even in winter.

Some birds fly to warmer countries in the winter and return the following year. This is called migration.

▲ Female birds have a patch of bare skin under their bodies. This mallard uses her body warmth to keep her eggs warm.

◀ Swallows breed in Europe and North America. In winter they migrate south to warmer countries. This swallow is drinking as it flies over a river.

▼ A thick layer of blubber and tightly packed feathers keep emperor penguins warm in the frozen Antarctic.

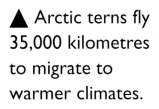

▲ Arctic terns fly
35,000 kilometres
to migrate to
warmer climates.

This bee-eater is 'gaping' to cool ▶
itself. It may die if it gets too hot.

A bird cannot sweat to lose
body heat as most mammals
do. It can cool itself by sitting
with its beak open, 'gaping'.

Birds that live in deserts and other very hot regions rest in the shade during the hottest part of the day.

▼ A heron spreads its wings to cast a shadow over the nest to keep the eggs cool.

How to keep warm and cool

- Black-necked storks spray their eggs with water to cool them.
- Birds living in cities cool themselves in pools and fountains.

Getting around

Most birds use their wings to fly. When a bird flaps its wings, the flight feathers in the wings push against the air. This lifts the bird off the ground and pushes it forward.

▼ The wings of a wandering albatross measure 3.3 metres from the tip of one to the tip of the other. The albatross can glide for hours without flapping its wings.

A hummingbird ▶
hovers by beating
its wings 70 times
a second. It needs
to hover so that it can sip
nectar from flowers.

Small birds have short
wings that they must
flap very quickly.
Birds with larger wings flap slowly and
can glide to save their energy.

▼ Penguins use their flipper-like wings to swim underwater.

The double-wattled ▶ cassowary cannot fly. It escapes predators by running. It can also swim across rivers.

Ways of moving

- Birds that fly have lightweight bones.
- A bird uses its tail for steering.
- Emperor penguins toboggan along the snow on their tummies.
- Mute swans run along the water to take off.
- The flightless ostrich can run at 70 kilometres per hour.
- Swifts spend most of their life in the air, including sleeping in short naps.

There are about fifty types of bird that cannot fly. Many of these have developed large powerful legs for running.

Flightless birds may have lost the ability to fly because they no longer needed to fly to find food or escape from danger.

▼ The roadrunner rarely flies. It uses its wings for balance to run after prey at up to 40 kilometres an hour.

Hatching and rearing chicks

Male and female birds come together to breed and raise their young. Some birds sing a courtship song to attract a mate. Others perform a complicated dance.

▼ These Japanese red crowned cranes are performing a courtship dance. They will probably stay together for life.

▲ A female blackbird brings food for her young. The chicks are born with few feathers so they cannot fly.

Most birds lay their eggs in a nest. This may be a simple pile of twigs or a neat, carefully woven nest.

Young swans, called cygnets, follow their ▶ parents soon after hatching. The adult swans teach the cygnets how to survive.

◀ Plovers nest on the ground. This golden plover pretends it has a broken wing to lure a predator away from its nest.

There are many predators on the look-out for eggs or chicks. Parent birds have to keep a constant watch and will fight off raiders.

▼ Cuckoos lay their eggs in other birds' nests (inset). This little reed warbler is trying to feed the huge cuckoo chick she has reared.

Unusual nesting places

- Some types of penguins nest in old rabbit burrows.
- The male parent emperor penguin looks after the egg while the female feeds in the sea. He balances the egg on his feet to keep it off the snow.
- European wrens may nest in garden sheds.
- Mallards sometimes nest in hollow trees.

▼ White storks often build their nests on high rooftops, such as churches.

Some birds nest in large colonies, making it harder for predators to attack. However, squabbles often break out between neighbours.

Caring for pet birds

- Make sure your cage has plenty of space.
- Provide the correct food and water.
- Remember that birds kept on their own need human company.
- Many birds enjoy a spray of fine water.
- Provide a supply of food and water in the garden for wild birds, especially during cold weather.

Birds are often kept as pets, but they need special care. You can study the characteristics of birds by looking closely at pet birds.

Pet budgies ▶ should be kept in a cage with plenty of space, or in an outdoor aviary. In the wild, they live in large flocks.

Birds need to fly. When they are young, they can be trained to fly around the room and then return to their cage.

▼ A bird feeder with nuts will attract wild birds, like these great and blue tits, to visit your garden.

Cockatoos make good pets. ▶ Like budgies, they should have plenty of space and company. Pet cockatoos can mimic human words.

Unusual birds

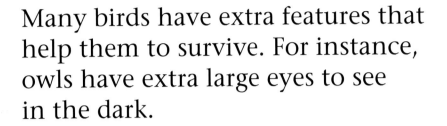

Many birds have extra features that help them to survive. For instance, owls have extra large eyes to see in the dark.

▼ The secretary bird looks like an eagle on stilts. It kills large prey, such as snakes, by stamping on them.

Some birds have unusual habits. Oxpeckers ride on the backs of large grass-eating animals. They feed on the parasites and flies living on the animal's skin, helping to clean the animals at the same time.

▲ Pelicans plunge their heads underwater, catching fish in their net-like beaks.

Unusual features

- Pelicans have a beak pouch to store fish.
- A sword-billed hummingbird's beak is as long as its body.
- Hoatzin chicks have claws on their wings for climbing trees in their rainforest home.

The scale of birds

Human   Ostrich   Bird of Paradise   Snowy Owl   Stilt   Bald Eagle   Peregrine Falcon   Vulture

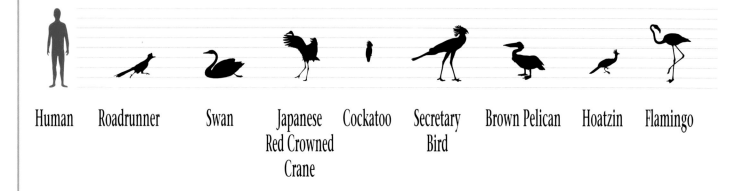

Human   Roadrunner   Swan   Japanese Red Crowned Crane   Cockatoo   Secretary Bird   Brown Pelican   Hoatzin   Flamingo

Human   Fulmar   Mallard   Emperor Penguin   Arctic Tern   Heron   Black-necked Stork   Wandering Albatross   Double Wattled Cassowary

| Bee-eater | Hummingbird | Swift | Blackbird | Golden Plover | Human Hand |

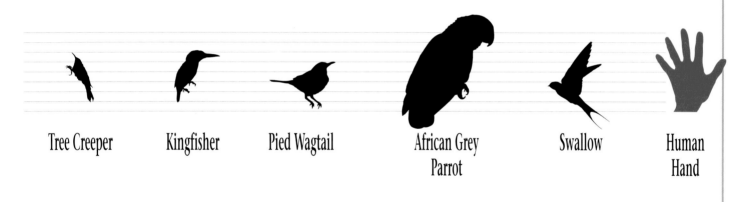

| Tree Creeper | Kingfisher | Pied Wagtail | African Grey Parrot | Swallow | Human Hand |

| Cuckoo | Reed Warbler | Budgerigar | Oxpecker | Woodpecker Finch | Wren | Human Hand |

Topic Web

SCIENCE

Classification.

Growth and reproduction.

How birds adapt to their environment.

Food chain.

Predators and prey.

GEOGRAPHY

Bird habitats – forests, grasslands, deserts, lakes, rivers, seashores.

Migration routes.

MATHS

Compare and measure different birds' sizes.

Work out how many kilometres migrating birds fly.

ART/CRAFT

Make a collage. or paint a mural showing birds in their habitats.

Birds
Topic Web

DANCE/DRAMA

Mime a baby chick in the nest.

Show the baby growing up, leaving the nest and flying away.

ENGLISH

Write about a day in the life of a chosen bird.

Activities

Science Study birds by attracting them to your school playground or garden. Put out different kinds of food, such as brown bread crumbs, seeds, nuts and water. Look at how the different birds feed. Look at their different beaks. Record the different kinds of food each type of bird eats.

Geography Look in a library to find out the names of birds that migrate to your country. What countries do they come from? Why do they leave those countries and come to yours? Draw a map of the world. Draw lines to show the migration routes taken by the birds.

English Imagine you are a swallow flying from South Africa to where you live. Write a story of your journey. What do you see? What happens on the way?

Art/Craft Make a collage of a bird. Cut out the feathers from coloured paper and stick them on so that they overlap. Tissue paper or similar is best. The wings and tails will have larger, longer feathers

Dance/Drama Improvise a dance or mime a chick hatching out of the egg. First be the chick curled up in its egg; then peck your way out as you hatch. Be a newly-hatched chick with closed eyes, fed by its parents. As your feathers grow, stretch your wings and finally fly away.

Maths Use the scale on pages 28–9 to compare the sizes of different birds with each other and with you, or with your hand. Are any birds bigger than you? Work out how many kilometres migrating birds fly.

Glossary

Antarctic The frozen area at and around the South Pole.

Arctic The frozen area at and around the North Pole.

Aviary A large outdoor enclosure for keeping birds.

Blubber The fat of penguins and sea animals.

Camouflaged Coloured or patterned like the surroundings to help hide from predators.

Courtship Spending time with an animal of the oppposite sex just before mating.

Habitats The natural home of plants and animals.

Hover To stay suspended in the air without moving forward.

Migration In the case of birds, moving from one country to another to escape cold winters or hot summers.

Nectar A sugary substance produced by plants to attract insects.

Parasites Animals (or plants) that live and feed off others.

Polar regions The areas around the North and South poles.

Predators Animals that hunt others for food.

Prey Animals that are hunted for food.

Warm-blooded Refers to animals whose body temperature stays about the same and is warmer than the surrounding air temperature. The skin may become hotter or colder, but the body temperature does not change.

Finding out more

Books to read

A First Look at Birds by Angela Royston (Belitha Press, 1998)

How to Look After Your Pet: Birds by Mark Evans (Dorling Kindersley, 1999)

Natural World: Penguin (Wayland, 2000)

Observing Nature: Seagull by Stephen Savage (Wayland, 1994)

The Wayland Book of Common British Birds by Nick Williams (Wayland, 1994)

Videos and CD Roms

Eyewitness: Bird A title in a series of natural history videos using nature photography combined with graphics and special effects. (Dorling Kindersley, 1997)

Eyewitness Encyclopedia of Nature: a multimedia reference guide to the natural world. (Dorling Kindersley, 1998)

The Life of Birds by David Attenborough (BBC Videos, 1998)

Index

Page numbers in **bold** refer to photographs.

Picture Acknowledgements:
Bruce Coleman /J. & P. Wegner cover (inset), /Andrew Purcell 4, /Scott Nielson 6, /Mike McKavett 7(l), /Hans Reinhard 7(r), /Paolo Fioratti 8(t), /Kim Taylor 8(b), /Leonard Lee Rue 9,11, /Gordon Langsbury 14(t), /Wayne Lankinen 17(t), /C. & D. Frith 18, /Steven Kaufman 20, /Kim Taylor 21(t), /George McCarthy 22(b), /John Markham 22 (b inset), /Eckart Pott 23, 26, /Kim Taylor 25(l), /John Cancalosi 25(r) and title page (r), /Marie Read 27; FLPA /Bob Langrish 19; NHPA /Bruce Beehler 5, /Stephen Dalton 10(t) and contents page, /John Shaw 10(b) and title page, /N.R. Coulton 12, /Stephen Dalton 13(t), /B. & C. Alexander 13(b), /Alan Williams 14(b), /Vincente Canseco 15, /Bill Costner 16, /Gerard Lacz 17, /Rich Kirchner 22(t); Oxford Scientific Films © Heinz Schrempp/Okapia 24; Tony Stone Worldwide /Art Wolfe cover (main pic); Wayland Picture Library 21(b).